WOW! I'M A WHALE!

A SWOPPERS STORY
by Tony Bradman

B Bloomsbury

340080

For all of
Cunningham's little treasures,
big and small

First published in Great Britain in 1996
Bloomsbury Publishing Limited, 38 Soho Square, London W1V 5DF

The moral right of the author and illustrator has been asserted
A CIP catalogue record of this book is available from the British Library

ISBN 0 7475 2655 9 pb
ISBN 0 7475 2654 0 hb

Printed and bound in Great Britain by
Clays Ltd, St Ives plc

10 9 8 7 6 5 4

Contents

A small cloud of gas drifts towards a lonely cove…
It shimmers, and gives off an eerie glow.
Where it came from is a mystery. Perhaps it has
travelled across the unimaginable chasms of space.
Perhaps it is the product of a secret laboratory…
Whatever the truth, one thing is certain. Any
child who meets it is in for an amazing experience,
as a particular boy is about to discover.
Follow him as he tumbles into the weird, wild
and wonderful world of . . . **Swoppers!**

CHAPTER ONE

A Storm Brewing

'Hey, Dad!' yelled Nathan Jones from the kitchen at the top of his voice. He put two brimming bowls of cereal on the table, poured hot coffee into a big mug and orange juice into a smaller one, then sat down. *'Breakfast!'*

'Coming!' Nathan heard his father yell back. Heavy footsteps trudged out of the bathroom, down the stairs and along the hall to the kitchen. The door opened and his dad walked in. He sat opposite Nathan, and smiled.

'You needn't have gone to all this trouble, Nathan,' he said, nodding at the neatly laid place settings, the cereal, the toast, the coffee. 'I'm very impressed, but shouldn't you be getting ready for school?'

'No, Dad, I shouldn't,' said Nathan, patiently. 'Don't you remember? I told you yesterday, school doesn't start again till next week.'

'I'm sorry, Nathan,' said Dad, looking embarrassed. 'I know I'm a bit forgetful at the moment. But I've got such a lot on my mind...'

Nathan sighed. Actually, he thought as they ate, Dad had been pretty distracted for the last month. He couldn't blame his father for being in a state, though. Nathan was worried about what was happening himself.

Nathan lived alone with his dad in a small town by the sea. Dad owned a boat, and made a living by taking tourists on whale-watching trips. Each spring and summer the whales visited the feeding grounds offshore.

Nathan could understand why people flocked from all over the world to see them, too. There was nothing to compare with the sight of a colossal humpback leaping through the waves right in front of you.

But this year everything had changed. For some unknown reason, the whales were staying away. April, May and June went by, then July, and now it was

August, and so far hardly a single whale had been spotted...

No whales meant no tourists, of course. No tourists meant no whale-watching trips. No whale-watching trips meant no money coming in. And no money coming in had made Nathan's dad an anxious man.

Nathan hated seeing his dad this edgy. But you can't really help with most grown-up stuff when you're only a kid. That's why Nathan had made breakfast. At least he'd felt like he was doing *something* useful.

'Are there any chores you want me to do today, Dad?' he said.

'Good of you to offer, Nathan,' said Dad. 'But no, I don't think so. I've got some stuff to take care of down at the harbour, and I'll be back in time to make us both dinner. By the way, has the mail arrived?'

'There was *one* letter...' said Nathan, reluctantly.

Nathan had deliberately not mentioned the official-looking envelope he'd found on the doormat. The only letters they'd been getting recently were from the bank, and they usually made his dad very nervous.

'You'd better hand it over,' said Dad, grimly.

Nathan pulled the letter from behind the toaster and passed it across. He watched his dad rip open the envelope, unfold the contents, and move his eyes swiftly down the lines. Nathan could tell it wasn't good news.

'What is it, Dad?' he asked, although he didn't really want to know.

'The bank manager says he can't let us borrow any more money,' Dad replied. 'If things don't start improving soon, I'll have to sell the boat and find a shore job. I could try that new factory up the coast, I suppose . . .'

'But you'd *hate* working in a factory, Dad!' said Nathan. He knew his dad loved being his own boss, *and* that he loved the sea even more.

'I have to make a living somehow, Nathan,' said Dad, gently. He stood up, took the bowls to the dishwasher, and peered out of the window. 'I don't like the look of those clouds,' he said. 'Could be a storm brewing.'

'I just wish there was something *I* could do to help,' said Nathan.

'There's not much you *can* do,' said Dad, turning to ruffle Nathan's hair. Then he smiled. 'Not unless you know where Cunningham's Treasure is. A chest full of pirate gold would take care of our debts quite nicely.'

'Some hope, Dad,' Nathan replied. He'd never be able to find any treasure, not in a million years. Nathan was *dead* sure about that.

Which just goes to show how wrong you can be...

CHAPTER TWO
Gloom and Doom

Nathan waved goodbye as his dad drove off, then wheeled his bike from the garage. That letter had left him feeling thoroughly fed up. He didn't want to watch TV or play on his computer. He *had* to get out.

He whizzed down the street and into town. It was quiet for a summer day at the peak of the tourist season. That probably had a lot to do with there being absolutely *no* tourists around, Nathan thought unhappily.

Still, there were plenty of people to say hallo to. Everybody who lived and worked in the town knew Nathan, and liked him. Each person he passed greeted him, and the drivers of several cars tooted cheerfully.

'Morning, Nathan!' said Mr Johnson, the man who ran the 7-Eleven store. He was putting copies of the local newspaper in a rack. 'See this?' he said, pointing to the front pages. 'Maybe things will start to improve!'

'Morning, Mr Johnson,' Nathan replied, stopping to glance at the headlines. It seemed the government was sending a party of scientists to the area to discover why the whales hadn't appeared this year.

'I wouldn't count on it if I were you, Wendell,' said Mrs Camaro, who ran the doughnut store next door. 'It might take them *years* to come up with an answer. I'll bet they don't even know where to start looking.'

'You shouldn't be so full of gloom and doom, Maria,' said Mr Johnson.

Nathan silently rode away as Mr Johnson and Mrs Camaro began to argue. The whole town was affected by what was happening, so inevitably the whale problem tended to be the main topic of adult conversation. Nathan had heard it all before. He didn't want to hear it again.

His tyres hummed along the empty beach road. At one end was the harbour, but at the other, in the direction Nathan was heading, there was a place called Buccaneer Cove. It was Nathan's favourite spot.

He had even done a special project at school about it, so he knew how the cove had acquired its name. Captain Cunningham the buccaneer had used it as his secret base for years during the eighteenth century.

His enemies had tracked him down in the end, and he had tried to escape with his hoard of treasure. Then a terrible gale just off the coast had sent his ship and its crew straight to the bottom of the ocean.

That was the legend, at any rate. Nobody had ever found the ship, although a couple of expeditions had dived in search of it. But Nathan was sure Cunningham's Treasure *did* exist, and was still out there, somewhere.

Nathan reached the end of the beach road, stopped, and got off his bike. In front of him was the cove, a deserted curve of sand with a sea-wall behind it, and an old jetty jutting far out into the bluey-green ocean.

He propped his bike against the sea-wall and walked down the jetty. He leaned on a railing and thought of all the fun he'd had at Buccaneer Cove in the past, just mooching around or pretending to be a pirate.

But with things as bad as they were, it was hard to have any fun at the moment. Nathan wished he could find Cunningham's Treasure for his dad. Then his dad wouldn't be forced to get a job in that new factory.

Nathan sighed. He felt so helpless! If only the whales would return, he thought longingly as he stared into the softly lapping water. He let his mind fill with images of humpbacks leaping and rolling in the waves...

And that's when a certain small gas cloud descended on him.

At first Nathan assumed it was nothing more than a stray patch of passing sea-mist. Thick fogs often drifted inland here without warning. Then he noticed this particular sea-mist was rather different from usual.

It swirled, and glowed with an eerie light, and shimmered, and seemed to coil around him, almost as if it were alive... Nathan began to feel slightly uneasy, and wondered if he should think about moving.

But it was too late for that.

Suddenly Nathan went rigid from his head to his toes, and fell backwards like a toppled tree. His insides were full of the strangest, most peculiar sensation, and his skin had started to tingle as well.

Nathan didn't panic. Not until he started to expand, that is...

CHAPTER THREE

An Enormous Splash

Nathan felt his shoulders and rear end scraping over the rough planks of the old jetty, while his feet remained stationary. From the corners of his eyes he glimpsed the railings flashing past in a blur of speed.

There was a *WHOOSHING* sound, too, followed by a succession of splintering noises, and the groan of old timber under huge strain. Nathan wanted to shout for help, but his voice seemed to have vanished.

That was the least of his problems, however. Either he had gone mad, he thought... or somehow he had been pumped up to *colossal* size.

There was worse to come. The tingling grew stronger, and stronger, and stronger. Nathan could sense his legs being melted together, his arms flattened, his head stretched and squashed into his neck...

Then his eyes seemed to slide into his ears, and

Nathan felt sick.

He barely heard the *FLAP! FLAP!* as his feet turned into flukes, and the *SMASH! SMASH!* as his flippers hit the railings. But he *did* hear more splintering noises, more timber groans, and a final, ominous *CRACK!*

Suddenly, the jetty collapsed.

Nathan crashed into the sea with an enormous *SPLASH!*, and lay in a chaos of foam and bubbles and

broken wood. He tried to gather his wits, but there wasn't time. Nathan realised he was starting to sink.

He tried hard to stay on the surface, but no matter how much he writhed and strained, his body refused to do what it was told. Nathan was stumped. His brain didn't seem able to send the right signals any more.

So Nathan sank... and sank... and sank.

OK, he thought. What did he do now? The answer came to him the instant he asked the question. He simply had to stop panicking. If he relaxed, his natural buoyancy should take him back to the surface.

It was a lot easier thought than done, but Nathan knew he didn't have a great deal of choice. He set about emptying his mind of everything except the idea of being calm, of being completely relaxed, of *floating...*

And gradually, it began to work. To his relief, Nathan stopped going down, and soon he felt himself rising. It seemed to take for ever, but eventually he bobbed into the air and sunlight, and breathed out.

A loud, wet, *SNORT!* startled him, and he looked round wildly to find its source. He twisted one way, and then he twisted the other. But all he could see was a long, knobbly, dark-grey shape in the water.

A shape he seemed to be attached to. A shape that reminded him of... No, it couldn't be, thought

Nathan. This *had* to be a dream. He must still be at home in bed, he hadn't woken up yet, he hadn't made breakfast...

But it was all so... well, so... *real*.

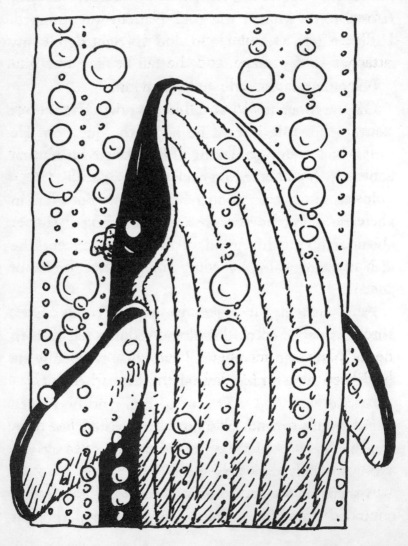

Nathan twisted to look again at the shape stretching behind him. As he did, a gigantic tail emerged majestically from the water and slapped hard on the waves. Spray leapt high into the air, and Nathan shot forward.

There was absolutely no doubt about it. He *was* attached to the shape, and the tail belonged to him, too. Nathan had actually felt it moving.

'*Wow! I'm a whale!*' he thought. A young humpback, to be precise!

It was incredible, but it did make some kind of sense. It explained that feeling of expanding to a colossal size, the old jetty collapsing under the increase in weight, that loud snort Nathan had been startled by.

Nathan realised he must have made the noise himself.

After they surfaced, whales always breathed out through the small blowholes on the tops of their heads. Nathan remembered hearing them do it when he'd been helping his dad on the boat during school vacations.

But wait a second, Nathan thought. This *had* to be impossible. It would be unbelievable even in an episode of *The Outer Limits*. There was nothing on Earth that could turn somebody into a whale. Or was there?

Nathan pictured the weird, shimmering mist that had descended on him from nowhere. Suppose it had been some kind of toxic, radioactive cloud which could transform you into what was in your mind at the time?

Maybe he should have stayed at home after all, he thought, miserably...

CHAPTER FOUR
One in a Zillion

Nathan drifted in the waters of Buccaneer Cove, horrified by his sudden transformation. Then the panic came rushing back, filling his mind with fear, and immediately he felt himself starting to sink again.

Down, down, down he went, deeper than before, down into the ocean, the panic growing inside him until he thought he might burst. But he didn't, he just kept silently sinking further down, and down, and down...

Get a grip on yourself! he thought, desperately.

Nathan knew whales could spend long periods submerged. But he also knew they were mammals, and that they needed to breathe air eventually. So he had to get back to the surface. Otherwise he would simply drown.

It would probably take ages, too, and that didn't seem like a very pleasant way to die. In fact, imagining it made Nathan's panic even worse, which didn't help matters. He started to sink even faster.

OK, he thought. If he was a whale, then he *must* be able to swim. It was what whales did, wasn't it? And

they did it by
moving their flukes,
rather as human swimmers
moved their legs in the butterfly
stroke.

Nathan had already been given a demonstration of what his rear could do without him directing it. He realised he just needed to get it under control. So he concentrated on sending the correct message to his tail.

The result was amazing.

Nathan felt himself powering upwards. He went faster, and faster, and faster, and within a few seconds he was bursting into the light again. And to his great surprise, he leapt through the air in a graceful arc, turned... Then *CRASHED!* on his back with another enormous *SPLASH!*

What a rush! he thought as he rolled right way up

and snorted air and spray out of his blowhole. It had been the most exhilarating feeling Nathan had ever experienced, miles better than the best water slide.

He swam forward a little, concentrating on keeping his speed under control, and getting used to steering with his large flippers. He went in a circle, did a figure of eight, dived, surfaced, and came to a halt.

Nathan felt happier now he knew he could handle this huge new body of his. He wasn't going to drown just yet. It was time to take stock.

He raised his massive head above the waves to get a good view of what was left of the jetty. Focusing in a single direction proved rather difficult, however. It seemed Nathan could see almost the entire cove at once.

He realised that was because his eyes were actually looking in different directions. He remembered reading in a book his dad sold on his boat to the tourists that whales had a much wider field of vision than humans.

They couldn't see very well, though, Nathan thought. There was a lot of overlap, and it was fairly blurry, probably because of the sea-water draining off over his eyeballs. But he could just make something out...

With a shock, he saw that the gas cloud was still there. It was sitting shimmering on a lone post stand-

ing up in the water, almost like it had got stuck, somehow. But then perhaps it hadn't got stuck at all. Maybe it was waiting for him.

Nathan thought about it. If the gas cloud *had* turned him into a whale, he reckoned it might change him back. He could swim to it this instant, and let it touch him while he pictured himself as a human being.

It was certainly worth a try, he decided. He gave his tail a gentle flick and headed towards the cloud. In a few moments he might be on dry land, this whole crazy nightmare at Buccaneer Cove behind him forever.

But Nathan paused a few metres from that lone post. You could look at this freak accident from two angles, he suddenly realised. Of course, the obvious thing was to think of it as a disaster. In another way, though...

It could be a one-in-a-zillion chance to help his dad.

The ocean was the whales' home, wasn't it? They could swim and dive and explore practically anywhere they wanted to, couldn't they? That meant Nathan was now capable of searching for something very special.

He could find Cunningham's Treasure.

CHAPTER FIVE
Lost at Sea

It was a golden opportunity, thought Nathan. Then doubts came rushing into his mind, just as the panic had done before. What if he didn't find the treasure? What if the cloud disappeared while he was off searching? What if he was *never* changed back into a human being?

OK, that's enough what-ifs, thought Nathan, pushing the last one firmly into a remote corner of his mind. It was a possibility he wasn't willing to consider. Besides, he didn't want to start sinking for a *third* time.

Nathan swam a little closer to the gas cloud and examined it carefully with his nearest eye. He couldn't be absolutely sure, but it didn't seem to be moving from the post. It had been there for quite a time now.

The question was – how much longer would it hang around? Ten minutes? Half an hour? Nathan bobbed in the sea, almost hoping the cloud would show him some kind of sign. But it just sat there, glowing eerily.

Nathan made up his mind. He decided he could take a look on the sea-bed outside Buccaneer Cove, provided he returned fairly quickly. Even if the cloud did move while he was gone, it probably wouldn't get far.

At least, that's what he was hoping. Anyway, it wasn't every day you got the chance to be a whale, for heaven's sake! Nathan felt pretty sure it would be a lot of fun, and he could certainly do with a bit of that.

He gave a few quick flicks of his tail, circled the post, then headed towards the open ocean. He felt strangely as if he were starring in a scene from some incredible fantasy movie. But this was actually happening...

Nathan passed through the gap between the two headlands that enclosed the cove. The water was colder beyond, the waves larger and topped with foam. Soon they were sweeping over him, one after the other.

But Nathan wasn't afraid of the sea. Being the son of a sailor, he'd always lived close to it. He'd been going out on boats since before he could remember. His dad had taught him to be a good swimmer, too.

Swimming as a whale was very different, though. It felt so much more... well, the only word Nathan could think of to decribe the sensation was *natural*. This huge new body of his was perfectly adapted to the water.

Nathan surged through the waves, his giant flukes

powerfully beating up and down behind him. It was incredible. He seemed to cover an enormous distance, and however fast he went, he didn't get tired or out of breath.

After a few minutes he stopped to check on his position. The coast was still reassuringly visible, but it was now quite distant. Surrounding him was a wide expanse of bluey-green waves sprinkled with spray. It seemed as good a spot as any to begin a treasure hunt.

Nathan breathed in, lifted his huge tail, pointed his head downwards, and dived. At first he concentrated on descending slowly and steadily. But then he realised he was taking too long, and increased his speed.

Soon he was facing a serious problem. Sunlight penetrated the water just beneath the surface, but the deeper Nathan dived, the darker the depths became. After a while, all he could see below was blackness.

It was tough staying on course as well. The sea's temperature seemed to drop dramatically every few metres down, and Nathan was bewildered by the powerful currents pulling at him from several directions at once.

There was something else he couldn't quite work out. It was almost as if the water tasted slightly wrong, although Nathan realised he had no idea what it was supposed to taste like to your average marine mammal.

Suddenly Nathan *did* feel frightened. What the heck was he doing there? He must be out of his mind! He should never have left Buccaneer Cove and the cloud. He stopped, turned, and started heading upwards...

He burst into the air at last, and looked for the coast line. He swam in a circle, peering in every direction. But it was no use. He just couldn't see it. Those currents had obviously taken him a long way out. He was lost at sea, and he didn't know what to do.

'*HELP! SOMEBODY HELP ME!*' he screamed inside.

And to his immense surprise, somebody replied.

CHAPTER SIX
The Name's Drew

'Yo, big guy,' squeaked a high-pitched voice from near-by. 'You got a major problem, or what? You're definitely broadcasting on almost every available frequency there, anyway. That's plenty of sonar, brother.'

Nathan twisted round in the water to look at who was speaking. A small creature leapt clear of the waves, dived in, surfaced again, and raised its head to stare at him. Nathan could just see its tiny eyes and snout.

It was a dolphin, but Nathan had never encountered one so little before. He wondered if it were a miniature species he'd never heard of. Then he realised he had to make allowances for how he was seeing things now. He only *thought* it was small because he was so *big*!

'Hallo-o! Anyone at home in there?' sang the dolphin. 'I mean, I know you overgrown guys can be a mite slow, but this is ridiculous! Hey, wait a minute, I get it... this is your idea of a practical joke, right?'

'I only wish it was,' said Nathan, without thinking.

'Whoa, spread the news, he SPEAKS!' squeaked the

dolphin. It rose from the water, hopped rearwards on its tail, did a quick back flip, dived and popped up in the same place it had started. 'Anything to add, pal?'

'Well, I, er...' stammered Nathan in confusion.

He was amazed he and the dolphin were actually *talking* to each other.

Then he remembered something else he'd read in the book his dad sold to the tourists. Whales *did* make sounds. They had been recorded doing it. And it was thought that the sounds might be a form of communication.

Nathan knew dolphins made plenty of noise, too. He'd heard them often enough around his dad's boat. He'd also seen an excellent programme about scientists in California trying to decipher what they were saying.

So when he'd thought he had been screaming *inside*, maybe he'd been making some kind of whale sound, and this dolphin had simply picked it up. Whales and dolphins obviously spoke the same language.

But the dolphin had also mentioned 'sonar'. Nathan knew sonar was a means of finding objects under water by bouncing soundwaves off them and tracking the echoes. Wasn't that pretty... *technical* for an animal?

'Come on, big guy,' the dolphin squeaked, breaking into Nathan's train of thought. Nathan sensed real friendliness in the voice. 'Spit it out. I'll do my best to help you if I can. Us sea mammals should stick together.'

'You won't believe me,' said Nathan.

'I might,' said the dolphin. 'It can't hurt to try.'

Nathan hesitated. If *he* met someone who claimed to have been transformed into a whale by a mysterious gas cloud, he'd be off before they said another word. Maybe this dolphin would react in the same way.

Nathan decided he would just have to take that chance. He badly needed to tell somebody what had happened to him, even if they did end up thinking he was totally crazy. He couldn't hold it in any longer.

'OK... but will you promise not to interrupt until I've finished?' Nathan replied at last. 'You have to let me tell you the whole story.'

'It's a deal!' squealed the dolphin. 'I'm all ears. By the way, the name's Drew, and I'm just passing through. What do they call you, big guy?'

'Nathan,' said Nathan. 'Nice to meet you, Drew.'

The dolphin nodded, but didn't say anything. Nathan realised he was waiting for him to speak. Here goes... he thought, then launched into his tale. He talked, and he talked, and he talked. And Drew listened.

When Nathan fell into silence once more, Drew swam a little closer, looked him in the eye, and gave a low whistle. 'Whoa,' he said. 'Far out.'

'There you go, I knew it'd be a total waste of time,' muttered Nathan sulkily. 'Be honest. You don't believe any of it, do you?'

'But *of course* I do!' said Drew. 'Hey, I know the truth when I hear it. I'm a *dolphin*. And dolphins are sea creatures with plenty of smarts, not land-dwellers with less brains than an oyster. No offence meant, big guy.'

'None taken,' said Nathan, laughter bubbling inside him.

He was suddenly sure he and Drew would get along *very* well.

CHAPTER SEVEN
Sound Advice

'So the problem is simple,' said Drew. 'You're lost, right?' Nathan nodded. 'Worry no more, my heavy-weight friend,' Drew continued. 'You tell me where it is you want to go, and I'll do my best to take you there.'

'Great!' said Nathan eagerly. The relief was terrific. 'I need to reach a cove on the coast, with two head-lands and a jetty. Well, the remains of one, anyway... It shouldn't be far. I don't think I was under water long.'

'That's the part of your story I can't get my head around,' said a puzzled Drew. 'Correct me if I'm wrong. You dived, but you couldn't find the stuff you were looking for, this thing that's gonna save your dad...'

'Cunningham's Treasure,' said Nathan.

'Whatever,' said Drew. 'So why didn't you just make with the old echo one-two when you were down there? I know you can do it. You were sending out some serious sonar when I first picked up your signal.'

'You mentioned that before, didn't you?' said Nathan. It was his turn to be puzzled. 'Listen, I'm sorry, but I don't understand what you mean.'

'Sonar, the savvy sea-mammal's secret weapon,' said Drew. He rose, did a quick back flip, splashed and surfaced again. 'That old sonic magic, squeak and you shall see the deepest depths of the sea. Catch my drift?'

'Er... no,' said Nathan.

'Really?' said Drew, disappointed. He did a sort of dolphin shrug. 'Hey, I was forgetting you're a human being under that blubber. I guess some concepts are just too hard for you land-dwellers to grasp.'

Then another fact from that book his dad sold popped into Nathan's mind, something about whales using sound to track fish. They sent out high-pitched calls and the echoes told them where the shoals were.

Nathan also knew that's how his dad often found groups of whales when they were submerged. He did a sweep of the sea beneath the boat with sonar equipment, and scanned the results on a small screen.

'Are you telling me I can use *your* kind of... sonar?' he said.

'You *were* using it, big guy,' Drew replied. 'Maybe you didn't realise, though. I suppose tuning in could be tricky if you've never done it before. OK, Nathan, here's where I give you some sound advice...'

And that's precisely what it was, too. Drew told Nathan to dip beneath the waves, close his eyes, and simply sing the highest note he possibly could. Then

he had to concentrate on picking up the echoes.

Nathan followed Drew's instructions, and suddenly a faint picture seemed to pulse inside his head. Nathan sang another note, and there it was again... a kind of map, like the screen on his dad's control panel.

In a way, it was even more amazing than that leap he'd made. Every note Nathan sang produced echoes, and as long as he kept concentrating on them, each echo added more detail to the picture in his giant skull.

'That's *incredible*!' he said, surfacing at last. 'Thanks, Drew!'

'Don't mention it!' said Drew. 'All part of the service. OK, if you'd like to follow my flashing flippers, big guy, I'll take you to the coast...'

'Er... could you hold on a second?' said Nathan quickly as his friend turned to swim off. 'I'm not actually sure I want to leave just yet.'

'Hey, what happened to all that help-get-me-out-of-here stuff?' said Drew. 'I thought you were up against some kind of deadline.'

'I suppose I am,' said Nathan. 'I *do* have to get back to the cloud before it disappears. But now you've shown me how to search for stuff on the sea-bed, I might still have time to find Cunningham's Treasure...'

'Your call, pal,' said Drew. 'Either choice is cool with me.'

Nathan raised his great head and peered at the horizon. Those dark clouds his dad had noticed earlier seemed a little closer, and there was definitely the hint of a breeze. But he might only need five more minutes...

'You *will* come with me if I look for the treasure, won't you?' he asked.

'Will I?' squeaked Drew. 'Try and stop me!'

'OK, then,' said Nathan. 'Any idea where we should start?'

He just hoped this was a decision he wouldn't regret...

CHAPTER EIGHT
A Clue or Two

'Your guess is as good as mine,' said Drew. He flipped over, vanished under the water, then surfaced. 'It's a big ocean and I don't know it all. We could always mosey on down to the bottom and mooch around...'

'Sounds fine by me,' said Nathan.

'Okey-dokey,' said Drew. 'Now, you'll have to fill your lungs before we dive. Er... you *do* know how to take deep breaths, don't you?'

'Yes, Drew, I do,' said Nathan with a sigh. 'Can we get on with it?'

'Hey, just checking!' said Drew. He circled Nathan at high speed, then swept to a halt in front of him. 'How about a race?' he squeaked. 'Last one there is a fat lazy slowpoke. Catch me if you can, blubber-man!'

'No problem, shorty!' laughed Nathan.

Then he took a huge breath, and dived.

It was different this time. Nathan remembered to sing out his sonar signals as he descended into the darkness, and to concentrate on the echoes. Soon that picture formed inside his head and stayed there, pulsing.

He couldn't keep up with Drew, though. The dolphin moved incredibly fast, and within seconds Nathan's new friend was a tiny blip deep below him. Nathan wasn't worried so long as Drew was in view.

Not *that* worried, anyway.

'Yo, buddy, I was beginning to wonder if you were gonna show,' said Drew when Nathan finally reached the sea-bed. 'I don't think there's a whole lotta doubt as to which of us here is the fat lazy slowpoke...'

'You win,' said Nathan, and laughed. Then he realised he couldn't send out sonar signals while he spoke. But the map in his head only faded slightly, and another high-pitched pulse raised it to full strength again.

So he and Drew could speak to each other *and* still use their sonar! Nathan had always known whales and dolphins were pretty clever. But they were obviously far more talented than he could ever have imagined.

'OK, big guy,' said Drew as they moved off together. They swam side by side just above the ocean bottom. 'Tell me, what exactly are we looking for? You'd better give me a clue or two if I'm gonna be any help.'

'An old, sunken ship,' said Nathan as he scanned the lumpy, bumpy sea-bed ahead for the object of his search. He couldn't resist getting his own back a little. 'Er... you *do* know what one of those is, don't you, Drew?'

'Oh, ha ha, very funny,' said Drew. 'Yeah, Nathan, I do. I've seen plenty of them. I just wish you land-dwellers would keep your garbage where it belongs. You're too fond of dumping it on us sea-creatures.'

'Er... sorry, Drew,' said Nathan, suddenly feeling guilty for the sins of the entire human race. 'But you mustn't think we're all like that, especially not kids. I mean, most of us want to make sure the sea isn't polluted...'

'That's OK, Nathan, you don't have to apologise,' said Drew. 'I know you're one of the good guys. Hey, is that a sunken ship over there?'

It was, but it wasn't the wreck Nathan was looking for. It was nowhere near old enough, and neither were the others he and Drew came across.

They discovered a modern cargo ship, an oil tanker, and a battleship from the second world war. They also found piles of junk and mounds of garbage.

And Nathan noticed that strange taste in the water again...

He wondered if the garbage might be causing it, but he felt too guilty about the possibility to ask Drew. Then he spotted something on the picture inside his head which drove that particular concern from his mind.

It was a sunken ship... *with three masts!*

'Drew, this might be the one!' he said, suddenly excited.

'Yeah?' said Drew. 'What do we do now?'

'We take a closer look, that's what,' said Nathan.

He swam swiftly towards the wreck, beaming as many sonar signals at it as he could. The hull was thickly encrusted with

barnacles. But it *did* appear to have the shape of a vessel from the eighteenth century.

Nathan went right up to a large hole in the main deck. A hole that turned out to be already occupied...

CHAPTER NINE
Duel in the Depths

An incredibly long, thin tentacle came waving out of the dark hole and snaked towards Nathan. He recoiled instinctively, and watched as a second long tentacle emerged, then several shorter, thicker ones...

Nathan was pretty confused. He had realised he didn't have to beam any sonar at the tentacles. He could actually *see* them. They were giving off a strange, fuzzy blue glow that lit up the sea for some distance around.

More tentacles appeared out of the hole, and Nathan decided he really didn't like the look of them. It seemed Drew felt the same.

'Whoa, let's make foam, pal,' said the dolphin from behind him. 'I don't think we wanna be around when the rest of that thing arrives.'

'But what if it's got Cunningham's Treasure in there?' said Nathan, almost hypnotised by the motions of the undulating tentacles. 'I mean, you never know, it might be willing to tell us. It might be *friendly*.'

Then there was a loud rending sound as something burst through the hole. Ancient timber tumbled to the sea-bed, and a huge, glowing creature rose above them

like a weird alien beast in a scary science fiction movie.

Scary was definitely the right word. The creature had an oval head and a narrow body, to which the tentacles were attached. It had a beak, and its cold eyes were fixed on Nathan and Drew with a stare of pure evil.

'Friendly, huh?' said Drew. 'I *don't* think so...'

'Oh my God, what *is* it?' asked Nathan, appalled. 'And how come it's glowing? You never told me anything about creatures that glow.'

'That, my friend, is a giant squid,' muttered Drew. 'A genuine killer-diller. And I'm sorry, but I forgot to explain that a few of the guys who live this deep glow in the dark, OK? Satisfied? Can we go now? *Please!*'

'You won't be going anywhere,' said a growling, gravelly voice. Nathan could feel a tight knot of fear forming inside his stomach. 'In fact,' continued the voice, 'you're both about to die. In terrible agony, probably.'

The giant squid swayed a little closer.

'I think we'll pass on that, if it's all the same to you,' said Drew. He leaned over and whispered to Nathan. 'Time to get your rear in gear, big guy. When I say the word, it's hi-ho and away we go. Ready? OK... hit it!'

Drew turned in a swirl of bubbles and frantically sped off. Nathan tried to follow, but he'd left it just a

fraction too late. He caught a glimpse of a colossal blue mass moving incredibly quickly through the water...

And the giant squid CRASHED! down onto him.

The force of the beast's charge pushed Nathan towards the ocean floor. He could feel the sheer strength of its tentacles as they wound round him, greedily fastening themselves onto his body with their horrible suckers.

The tentacles squeezed, and squeezed, and squeezed, and soon Nathan knew he was on the point of passing out. He heard a sharp clicking sound, and saw that vicious beak coming closer, and closer, and closer...

Then, just as his vision started to fade, a figure flashed past like a speeding missile, aiming directly at a spot between the squid's eyes.

It was Drew, and he'd come back to help. He THUDDED! into the giant squid, which grunted in pain and released Nathan. But a long tentacle lashed out, grabbed Drew, and dragged *him* down instead...

'Get outta here while you still can, Nathan!' squeaked Drew.

Nathan shakily pulled himself together, and watched as more tentacles curled round the struggling, squealing Drew. It was obvious the dolphin couldn't escape. It was also obvious he wouldn't last much longer.

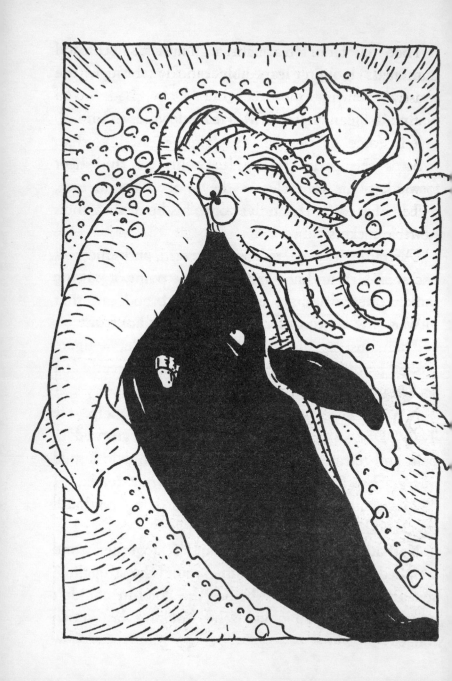

That knot of fear inside Nathan's stomach tightened. He didn't want a duel in the depths with a ghastly, glowing monster. But Drew had saved Nathan's life, and there was no one else around to save Drew.

So Nathan screwed up his courage... and shot forward.

'Leave... my... friend... alone!' he called out, powering faster and faster through the water. He SMASHED into the giant squid, propelling it backwards into the barnacle-encrusted hull of the sunken pirate ship.

What happened next was something of a surprise...

CHAPTER TEN
Tiny Sparkles

Nathan had expected the sunken ship to stay where it was. But he had rammed the giant squid so hard against it, the hull shifted. There was a terrible grinding noise as the freed keel scraped across some rocks.

The squid refused to loosen its grip on Drew, though. So Nathan pulled back for an instant, then rammed the evil beast even harder. He did it again, and again, and again, driving the squid – and the ship – before him.

At last the tentacles uncoiled, and Drew slipped from their grasp.

'Thanks, Nathan,' he said, weakly. 'I thought I was a goner there.'

Nathan didn't reply. He had been watching the giant squid in case of another attack. But it didn't seem very likely. The creature appeared to have been knocked out, and was hanging motionless in the water.

The sunken ship, however, was still moving.

Nathan looked beyond it, in the direction the vessel was travelling. Some distance further on he saw a

large, jagged crack in the sea-bed. Nathan suddenly felt extremely nervous about the ship's prospects.

He set off after it, and the closer he got to the crevice, the wider and deeper he realised it was. The ship moved steadily, relentlessly, onwards. Nathan soon realised he wasn't going to catch up with it.

He watched it tip over the crack's edge... and slide into the depths.

Nathan glimpsed a small, open chest fall through that hole in the main deck. It tumbled lazily in the ship's wake, faintly twinkling in the distant squid's blue light, spilling a trail of tiny sparkles into the water.

Then the darkness swallowed the lot... ship, chest and sparkles.

Nathan stared down, hopelessly. He knew he was poised above what scientists call a sea trench, an abyss too deep to be explored by human beings. So if that *had* been Cunningham's Treasure, it was lost for ever.

'And I'm the one to blame...' he murmured.

'Outstanding, big guy!' said a restored

Drew, swimming up beside him. Then he peered more closely at Nathan. 'You OK, pal?'

'No, I'm not,' said Nathan, miserably. 'Everything's gone wrong!'

'Whoa, am I hearing this?' said Drew. 'You fearlessly face up to the Evil Deep-Sea Strangler, pound him into mush, save your best buddy, and everything's gone *wrong*? Hey, you sure are hard to please.'

'I wasn't talking about fighting with that... that *creature*,' said Nathan, gloomily. 'Don't you see, Drew? I came here to help my Dad, and now I won't be able to. It's over. The treasure was our only hope.'

'Relax, Nathan,' said Drew softly. 'It's gonna be fine...'

'How could I have been so *dumb*?' exploded Nathan, angry with himself and ignoring the dolphin. 'I mean, it was stupid enough to imagine I could find the treasure in five minutes by mooching about on the sea-bed...'

'*With* some expert help, I might add...' said Drew.

'But what did I think I was going to do if I found it? Hah, tell me that!' said Nathan. Drew opened his mouth, but Nathan swept on. 'I don't exactly know where I am, do I? So how could I bring my dad here?'

'Well, I – ' Drew began.

'I couldn't, could I?' Nathan continued, fiercely. 'And even if I could, how would I explain it? Hi, Dad,

how was your day? What kind of a day did I have? Oh,
pretty ordinary, really, Dad, I got turned into a
whale...'

'Come on, big guy,' said Drew. 'Don't do this to
yourself.'

'...And I've found Cunningham's Treasure on the
sea-bed. Shall we go and get it?' said Nathan. He gave
a hollow laugh. 'He'd just tell me I'd been watching
too much TV. Unless he took me to a psychiatrist,
that is.'

'A what?' said Drew, confused.

'Oh, it doesn't matter, Drew,' said Nathan, his anger seeming suddenly to seep out of him in a large, unhappy sigh. 'It won't happen.'

'Shall I take you back to the cloud then, old buddy?' said Drew.

'There's no point,' muttered Nathan. 'I've been even more stupid about that. I'll bet it's long gone. I'll never, ever see my home again.'

'And neither will I,' growled a gravelly voice, groggily...

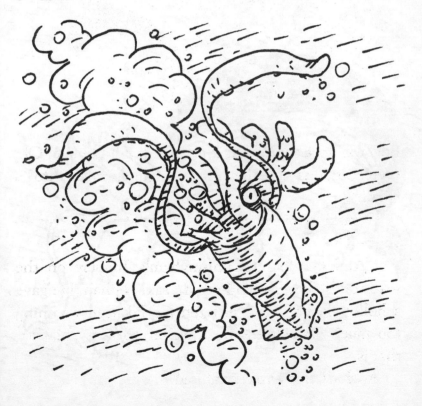

CHAPTER ELEVEN
An Invisible Substance

Drew instantly whipped round. Nathan turned more slowly, and saw... the giant squid! It had come to, and was floating behind them, its glow slightly faded. The beast still looked threatening, though.

'Back off, slime-ball,' snarled Drew. 'One word from me and my heavyweight pal will be happy to pick up where he left off.'

'Oh, *please*,' growled the squid. 'You don't seriously think that frightens me, do you? I was simply caught off guard by a pair of mean, sneaky cheats. Besides, I was out-numbered. I'd hardly call it a fair fight.'

'I don't believe I'm hearing this,' said Drew. 'First the guy ambushes us from a sunken ship, and now he's talking about fair fights.'

'Well, I won't be ambushing anyone from that particular wreck in future, will I?' snapped the squid crossly. 'Have you any idea how long I've lived in it, you vulgar little hooligan? Seventy-five years, *that's* how long!'

'Hey, then maybe it was time to find somewhere else to tuck your tentacles, Mr I've-Got-Too-Many-Legs,' Drew replied. 'If you ask me, it looks like the big guy did you a big favour. Ain't you gonna thank him?'

'Actually, I *was* thinking of moving,' said the squid, snootily. 'This neighbourhood is definitely not what it used to be. First we get a dreadful taste in the water, then common riff-raff like you start turning up...'

'The only riff-raff I see is *you*,' said Drew. 'And what *is* it with this taste? I might not be from here, but I noticed it straight off. Maybe it's you, wavy-brains. You're so ugly you're poisoning the water.'

'You mammals think you're so clever, don't you?' said

the squid. 'Well, you're not. It isn't me, but it *is* poison.
I'm surprised your fellow scoundrel can stand it. After
all, it's making most other whales stay away...'

'What did you say?' demanded Nathan, suddenly
alert and moving forwards. The squid retreated, its tentacles twitching with obvious terror. 'What poison?
And why is it keeping the whales away?'

'Leave me alone you... you *bully*!' squealed the squid.

'Hey, who are you calling a bully, you sad sack of

suckers?' said Drew. 'We were just protecting ourselves. *You* started the rough stuff.'

'Although I'*m* ready to finish it,' said Nathan, grimly. 'Now are you going to tell me what you're talking about? I'll count to three. One...'

'All right, all right,' said the squid, hurriedly. 'But you must be a pretty peculiar kind of whale if you don't know what's been going on...'

The squid then revealed some *very* interesting information. An invisible substance had recently begun to get into the water, something that could poison most sea creatures. Whales were especially vulnerable to it.

Apparently there was a faint taste of the stuff everywhere. But it was at its worst – and therefore most dangerous – in a particular place...

The whales' feeding grounds!

Nathan felt strange. He hadn't realised just how much he'd wanted to know *why* the whales hadn't come this year until the moment the squid had begun to explain the reason. It was like a secret door suddenly opening.

But the door had only opened half way. Now Nathan felt he wanted to push it back and see the whole truth at last. There was one final question which needed an answer before the story would be complete.

'So where is the poison coming from?' Nathan asked.

'I have absolutely no idea,' replied the squid.

'It could be something natural...' murmured Nathan.

'And it could be something *unnatural*,' said Drew. 'Look, Nathan, this kind of stuff doesn't get into the ocean unless it's put there by everybody's least favourite species. Are you tuning into me? Er, no offence, big guy...'

'None taken, Drew,' said Nathan, his mood lifting, his mind totally clear. 'You're right, it *must* be pollution. And I want to find the source.'

'Are you sure, Nathan?' said Drew. 'I mean, it could be risky...'

'I'm up for it if you are,' said Nathan.

'Hey, I might just tag along,' laughed Drew. 'Gimme some flipper, pal!'

Then the two friends swam off into the darkness...

CHAPTER TWELVE
Danger Dead Ahead!

'Good riddance, that's what I say!' they heard the giant squid calling out. The further Nathan and Drew swam away, the fainter the squid's voice – and blue glow – became. 'I hope the poison chokes the pair of you...'

'Ever had the feeling you're not too popular?' said Drew.

'Funny you should mention it,' said Nathan. 'I just have.'

They burst into laughter, and raced to the surface.

They were still laughing when they leapt clear of the waves. Nathan blew a huge *SNORT!* from his blowhole, then took a deep breath. It was a treat to be in the sunlight and fresh air after all that murkiness.

Those storm clouds were slightly closer, though, and the wind was whistling over the white-capped wave tops. Nathan decided to pay no attention to the weather. It still made him feel a little uneasy, though...

'So tell me, big guy,' said Drew. He rose from the water, did a quick back flip, then popped up in front of Nathan again. 'What's the plan?'

'Well, if the poison is at its worst
in the whales' feeding grounds, maybe
we should start looking there,' said Nathan. 'And
the easiest way to find *them* is to trace the taste to
where it's strongest. Obvious, really.'

'Whoa, good thinking, blubber-man,' said Drew,
admiringly. 'Maybe a few of you land-dwellers have got
more brains than I thought.'

'I'll take that as a compliment,' said Nathan. 'Ready?'

'As I'll ever be,' said Drew. 'After you, old buddy.'

'OK,' said Nathan. 'Let's do it...'

They both lifted their tails, and plunged beneath
the surface.

Down they went, down into the darkness once more. They swam side by side along the bottom, and soon worked out in which direction the bad taste was strongest. They headed that way, using their sonar as before.

The taste grew steadily worse. They encountered no other living creatures, and noticed nothing unusual. But that was spooky in itself, and only made Nathan feel uncomfortable. Drew wasn't very happy either.

'Ugh, *yuck*,' he said eventually. 'This water is so *gross*, Nathan. I don't know if I can carry on. Not without losing my lunch, anyway.'

'Don't worry, Drew,' said Nathan. The taste was making him pretty nauseous too. 'You can stay here and wait for me if you want...'

'Hey... *YIKES!*' squealed Drew, suddenly. '*DANGER DEAD AHEAD!*'

The sheer panic in Drew's warning was enough to frighten Nathan. He froze, expecting some terrible

beast to leap on him just as the squid had done. But the seconds slowly passed, and nothing happened.

'Drew, what is it?' Nathan whispered.

'I only wish I knew, big guy,' Drew whispered in reply. 'I spotted something on the sea-bed, and I thought it was our old friend the Evil Deep-Sea Strangler coming back for a re-match. But it's just lying there...'

Nathan realised Drew was probably better at picking up detail than him, so he tried to narrow the focus of his own sonar map. He had already noticed the sea-

bed was beginning to rise in a series of sand banks.

Nathan remembered his dad explaining that the shallow sea over the sand banks had always been rich in plankton and fish during the spring and summer. That made them very good feeding grounds for whales.

Then Nathan spotted a long line, rather like one of the squid's thinner tentacles. Drew was right, though. It certainly wasn't moving.

The line stretched into the far distance in one direction, but came to an abrupt end in the other. There was something vaguely familiar about it, too. Nathan scanned his memory... and the answer came to him.

He and Drew had stumbled across a pipeline.

'Relax, Drew,' he said. 'It isn't dangerous. It's not even alive.'

'Oh yeah?' said Drew, suspiciously. 'What's it do, then?'

'That's difficult to explain,' said Nathan, trying to recall a film he'd been shown at school. 'People use things like this to send stuff from one place to another, I guess. It might be a gas, or a liquid of some kind.'

Nathan paused, and the word *BINGO!* flashed into his mind...

CHAPTER THIRTEEN
Full Circle

'Are you thinking what I'm thinking, old buddy?' muttered Drew, edging backwards. 'I mean, I don't wanna say I told you so, but it looks to me as if the stuff this particular thing is bringing might just happen to be – '

'The poison?' said Nathan. 'Got it in one, Drew.'

Nathan focused his sonar tightly on the small area surrounding the end of the pipeline. There was absolutely no doubt. A steady stream of liquid was flowing into the water. Nathan edged backwards as well.

'Any idea what it is, Nathan?' said Drew, nervously.

'Some kind of waste, I should imagine,' said Nathan unhappily.

'Oh, I get the picture,' said Drew. 'It's something you land-dwellers don't want, probably because it's *way* too dangerous. So you let it run into the ocean where only us dumb, *uncomplaining* sea creatures live.'

'I don't like it any more than you do, Drew,' said Nathan, softly.

'Hey, I know that, big guy,' said Drew with a sigh. 'It makes me mad, that's all. The sea is my *home*, and somebody is dumping this stuff in my back yard. And there doesn't seem to be a whole lot I can do to stop it.'

'We could always follow the pipeline,' said Nathan.

'What difference would that make?' asked Drew, bitterly.

'At least we'd know where the poison was coming from,' said Nathan.

'OK, Nathan,' said Drew. 'If you think it will do any good...'

He turned and swam off in a swirl of bubbles, and Nathan went after him. Nathan felt depressed. He wished he could stop the flow of poison for his friend, just as he'd wished he could solve his dad's problems.

Maybe, Nathan thought suddenly, maybe if he *could* find the original source of the poison, and maybe if the cloud was still there, then... forget it, Nathan told himself sternly. There was no point in dreaming.

He sped up, all the same.

The pipeline was very easy to follow. Their sonar showed it going in an unnaturally straight line across the sea-bed, and the further they moved away from the feeding grounds, the weaker the poisonous taste grew.

After a while Nathan noticed light penetrating the upper levels of the sea, and he realised the ocean floor had started to rise sharply. They were obviously getting near the coast. The pipeline's course didn't waver.

'I can't go in much closer, Drew,' he said finally. 'The water's getting too shallow. I don't want to end up stranded on a beach.'

'Hey, no sweat, big guy,' said Drew. 'I'll take over from here...'

Nathan watched his tiny friend swim ahead, his little flippers flashing through the murky water. He became a dot, then disappeared. Nathan waited anxiously for a few moments... then relaxed when Drew returned.

'Did you follow it all the way?' he asked.

'As far as I could,' said Drew. 'It goes into some rocks.'

'We might be able to see more from the surface,' said Nathan.

The two friends bobbed into the air. Nathan *SNORTED!* through his blowhole, and peered cautiously at the land in front of him.

He found himself looking at a small bay with the rocks Drew had mentioned on one side. The pipeline ran out of them and into a large building set back from the sea. Nathan recognised it immediately.

It was the new factory his dad had been talking about!

Nathan had seen it on a local news programme when it opened earlier this year. *Earlier this year*, he thought... and everything fell into place. They must have been pumping waste into the sea since the spring.

Nathan felt strangely as

if he'd come full circle. He knew what was keeping the whales away, and had traced it to its source. But he was still helpless. And he was almost full to bursting with frustration, as well!

'What now, old buddy?' asked Drew.

'I'm going to head for the cloud,' said Nathan, suddenly making up his mind. 'It *has* to be there. I've *got* to tell somebody what we've found!'

'You can tell us if you like,' said a rich, deep voice behind them.

Nathan turned... and was amazed by what he saw.

CHAPTER FOURTEEN
Whale Songs

A pair of humpback whales had surfaced in the sea behind them, and were spouting huge columns of spray through their blowholes. They were obviously adults, thought Nathan. They were totally awesome, too. Each was at least four times his size.

'Aren't you a tad young to be out on your own?' said the second whale. Just like a human grown-up talking to a child, thought Nathan. 'And what are you up to? Don't you know how dangerous it is around here?'

'Hey, excuse *me*,' squeaked Drew, leaping clear of the waves and splashing down in front of the whale who had just spoken. 'My big buddy *isn't* alone. And I'll bet we know more about what's going on than *you*.'

'Is that a fact?' said the whale with amusement. 'So you'll be aware this area is off-limits to sea mammals until it's safe again. We're just checking on the water quality, and warning anybody who gets too close.'

'Do you really know something?' said the whale who had spoken first, looking directly at Nathan. He suddenly felt shy, and nodded, hesitantly. 'Well then,' the whale went on. 'Don't you think you ought to tell us?'

'It's a long story,' said Nathan, nervously.

'Don't worry,' the whale replied in that rich, deep voice. It throbbed calmingly through Nathan's body. 'We have all the time in the world.'

Nathan knew *he* didn't, but he didn't want to hurry this, either. He had the oddest feeling these two whales would be able to help him, some-how. He just needed to convince them that what he had to say was true.

So once more Nathan took a deep breath, and talked, talked, and talked. Drew did too, chipping in with plenty of explanation and details, especially when Nathan got to the part where they encountered the giant squid.

'You poor things,' said the whale who had spoken first. She swam up to Nathan and gently nuzzled him with her snout. 'It must have been terrible, being attacked... I think you've been very brave. Both of you.'

'Does that mean you believe me?' asked Nathan.

'Why, *of course* we believe you,' said the other whale. He sounded

slightly offended. 'We're humpback whales, not...'

'Not land-dwellers with less smarts than an oyster?' asked Nathan.

'I wouldn't have put it *quite* that way,' laughed the whale.

'It's OK,' said Nathan. 'I've seen what the human race is doing. I'd just like the chance to stop this particular piece of pollution. And to do that, I need to return to the gas cloud. If it's still there, that is...'

'We'll find out for you,' said the whales, and sank slowly beneath the surface. Nathan was baffled and followed them, with Drew close behind.

'But how can you?' asked Nathan. 'It's not possible... is it?'

'Where these guys are concerned, old buddy,' whispered Drew, '*anything* is possible. They've got this amazing network. There are whales all over the ocean, pal. They keep tabs on *everything* that's happening.'

'You're kidding,' said Nathan.

'Trust me, Nathan,' said Drew. 'This will blow your mind.'

Suddenly Nathan heard an incredible sound, and realised it was the two whales singing. Soon the sea seemed filled with their haunting, beautiful whale songs. They sent them out... and the replies came singing back.

After a while, the whales fell silent, and rose to the

surface again. Nathan and Drew did the same, and waited to hear the report.

'Your cloud hasn't moved,' said the whale who had nuzzled Nathan. 'There's a similar team to us near your cove, and they noticed it.'

'But it won't be around much longer,' said the other. He raised his head above the water. 'There's a storm coming, and it's about to break...'

Nathan looked up himself. The whale was right. Those dark clouds were looming very close now, and the wind was whipping across the waves. Lightning flashed overhead, and thunder boomed.

'So that's it, then,' said Nathan, his mood darkening like the sky. 'I'll never make it back to the cloud before the storm blows it away.'

'I wouldn't give up just yet,' said the whale with the deeper voice...

CHAPTER FIFTEEN
A Wild Ride

'I don't see why not,' said Nathan, gloomily. He desperately wanted to cry, but he couldn't. 'There's nothing that can get me to Buccaneer Cove in the next few minutes. I'm going to be a whale for the rest of my life...'

'Not necessarily,' said the whale who had nuzzled him. 'This way.'

Both adult whales sank slowly beneath the surface once more. Nathan looked inquiringly at Drew, who simply did one of his dolphin shrugs.

'Beats me, pal,' said Drew. 'It's probably your only chance, though.'

Drew was right, and Nathan knew it. So he sank beneath the waves as well, and sped off after the whales, with Drew close behind him. The two grown-ups swam swiftly along the coast, then dived to the sea-bed.

'OK, now this is what we suggest,' said the humpback with the deeper voice. 'Just over there you'll find a rip-tide – a current that runs really fast. It should take you where you want, although it might be a wild ride...'

'Hey, what are we waiting for, old buddy?' squeaked Drew, happily. 'That sounds like it might be a whole bunch of fun, whatever happens.'

'Yeah, and a great end to a seriously weird day,' said Nathan, suddenly relaxing. 'I'm with you, Drew.' Nathan turned to the two whales. 'Thanks,' he said. 'And I promise I'll do my best to stop the poison...'

'We know you will,' said the whale with the deeper voice.

'Just take care,' said the other, and nuzzled him again.

Nathan nodded. Then he swam powerfully in the direction the adult humpbacks had indicated. Drew quickly came up beside him.

'Good luck!' Nathan heard the whales calling out. Then he spotted the current on his sonar, plunged into it, and was instantly swept away...

It *did* turn out to be a wild ride, wilder than the fastest, twistiest water-slide, or the whizziest, craziest roller-coaster. Nathan soon found himself barrelling through the .

darkness, unable to halt his headlong rush.

The current got faster and faster, and finally Nathan began to spin like a bullet. Then, just as he thought he couldn't take any more, he shot up and out of the waves, leapt through the air in a graceful arc, turned, and... *CRASHED!* on his back with an even bigger *SPLASH!* than before. If his first leap had been great, that one had been *fantastic*.

Nathan rolled right way up, and let off a *SNORT!* from his blowhole. In front of him were two familiar headlands, with a gap between. He hurried into Buccaneer Cove, eagerly searching for the gas cloud...

And there it was, still shimmering eerily on the lone post.

'Whoa, that was *some* current,' laughed Drew, surfacing beside Nathan. For a moment, Nathan had forgotten his friend. 'Hey, and it looks like you made it, big guy,' Drew continued. 'You gonna be OK, now?'

'I think so,' said Nathan. 'I'm pretty sure the cloud will change me back.'

'And will you tell your dad...' said Drew.

'About being a whale?' said Nathan. 'I guess not. I'll concentrate on the poison to begin with. I have to make him believe I've found out what's keeping the whales away. Then he can tell those government scientists.'

'You'll do it, Nathan,' said Drew. 'After today, old buddy, there's *nothing* you won't be able to do.

Although you'd better not hang around...'

They both looked up. The storm clouds had almost caught up with them, and the wind was beginning to flutter the edges of the gas cloud.

'So this is goodbye,' said Nathan. With a pang, he'd just realised what that word meant for their friendship. 'We might never meet again, Drew.'

'Maybe...' said Drew, sadly. Then he rose on his tail,

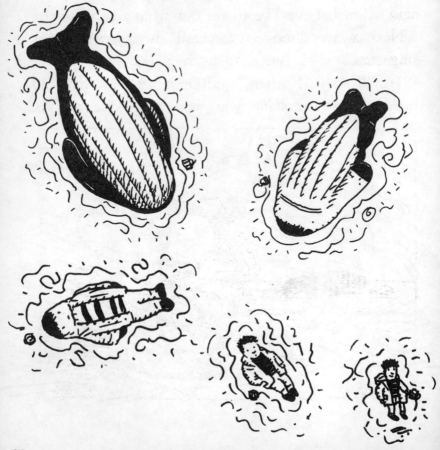

did a quick back flip, and sped off in a spray of white foam. 'But I wouldn't count on it,' he laughed. 'I'll be looking out for you, pal!' he squeaked... and was gone.

'And I'll be looking out for you, too,' said Nathan, softly.

He started swimming powerfully towards the gas cloud. He took careful aim, leapt from the water, remembered to fill his mind with images of himself as a boy, entered that swirling, glowing mist... and went rigid.

Nathan hoped the transformation wouldn't take too long this time. He had an *awful* lot to do.

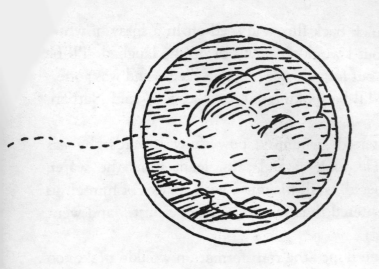

A small cloud of gas drifts away from a lonely cove...
And a boy bikes home happily to see his dad.
Where it will drift next is a mystery. Perhaps it
will waft its way silently, eerily out to sea.
Perhaps it will come shimmering down a country lane...
Whatever the truth, one thing is certain. Any
child who meets it is in for an amazing experience,
as one particular boy discovered. And next
time, it might be you tumbling into the weird, wild
and wonderful world of... **Swoppers!**